WHERE THERE'S A WILL THERE'S A WAY
一念岩をも通す

Ichinen iwa o mo tōsu

and other Japanese proverbs and sayings
with English equivalents

compiled by

Primrose Arnander   **Ritsuko Yamada Nishimae**

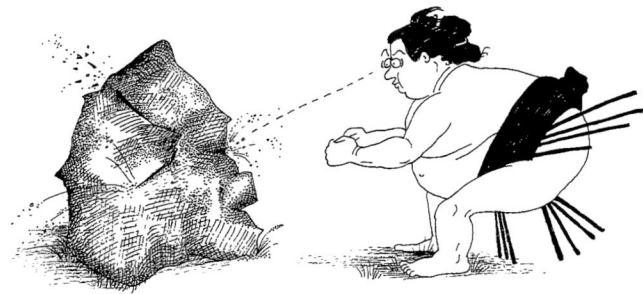

with illustrations by
Kathryn Lamb

WHERE THERE'S A WILL THERE'S A WAY
一念岩をも通す

Published by
Medina Publishing Ltd
310 Ewell Road
Surbiton
Surrey KT6 7AL
medinapublishing.com

© Primrose Arnander & Ritsuko Yamada Nishimae 2018
Illustrations © Kathryn Lamb 2018

ISBN 978-1-909339-99-6

All rights reserved. No part of this publication may be reproduced, stored in a retrieval system, or transmitted in any form or by any means, electronic, mechanical, photocopying, recording, or otherwise, without the prior permission of the copyright owners.

British Library Cataloguing-in-Publication Data
A catalogue record for this publication is
available from the British Library

Printed and bound by Interak Printing House, Poland

ROMAJI TRANSLITERATION

Romaji is a system of transliteration of Japanese script into the Roman, or Latin, alphabet, to facilitate the understanding of Japanese. This alphabet is used for the languages of two thirds of the world's population, in dozens of countries from Australia to Zimbabwe. To compress the thousands of characters of Japanese script into the standard Latin alphabet of 26 characters presents a formidable challenge.

Romaji's roots go back to the 16th century when Portuguese missionaries introduced Christianity into Japan. However, the Christians were banished from Japan in the early 17th century and there was no further development of romaji until the late 19th century. Since then, several versions of romaji have appeared. Romaji is now taught to schoolchildren in Japan and is an important tool in facilitating the relationship between Japanese and foreigners.

However, the written and spoken word are still not reconciled. Inflexion and rhythm play a large part in the Japanese language; therefore, the authors can give no guarantee that, if their English speaking readers recite a proverb in romaji to a Japanese friend, it will necessarily be immediately understood! It is hoped that they succeed in achieving a recognizable approximation and they will surely be congratulated for making the effort.

Each proverb is expressed in four ways:

1]	In Japanese characters	一石二鳥
2]	*Transliterated into romaji*	*Isseki nichō*
3]	English literal translation	Two birds with one stone
4]	English equivalent proverb	To kill two birds with one stone

AUTHOR'S PREFACE 1

It is over thirty years since the first book in this series of illustrated, bilingual, proverbs and sayings was published in 1985 and, since then, 'much water has flowed under the bridge'.

'The Son of a Duck is a Floater' (a proverb equivalent to the English 'Like father, like son') was the title of the first of three books of Arabic (and English) proverbs, collected by me and my late collaborator, Ashkhain Skipwith, while living in Jeddah, Saudi Arabia. They were illustrated by the now celebrated cartoonist, Kathryn Lamb, who was as familiar with everyday life in the Middle East as we both were.

The idea was that the book should not be too detailed and scholarly, but rather be an amusing gift from guest to host, in lieu of the more conventional bunch of fresh flowers. It was fascinating to collect and compare the myriad sayings and adages, hard sometimes to dignify them with the word 'proverb', that flow so readily from the lips of people of all countries as they go about their daily lives. Some echo the same sentiments, some are startlingly different, but gradually the preoccupations of a society emerge and… well, humans will be humans and there are, it would appear, as many similarities as differences between the desires and utterances of a populace.

This Japanese proverbs book is my fifth proverbs book. 'The Son of a Duck is a Floater' was followed by two more Arabic books with Ashkhain. In 2010, I joined forces with Marie-Hélène Claudel-Gilly to produce a French collection 'Don't Toss Granny in the Begonias'. French cartoon drawings came easily to the inventive Kathryn, but she faced more of a challenge when presented with the opportunity to illustrate my planned Japanese proverbs book, inspired by my close friend Noriko Barrow, as neither Kathryn nor I had ever lived in Japan.

It was a great boon for me when Ritsuko Yamada Nishimae arrived in London with her husband. Coming from America, where she trained as a psychotherapist, she was ideally placed to understand the subtle differences between apparently similar proverbs in the two languages and to appreciate the humour that underlay the project.

Confabulations were long and detailed between us, but despite a change of publisher and Ritsuko's return to Japan, we soon found that a finished book had taken shape. We hope that it will appeal both to Japanese and English speakers, but inevitably some will feel that this or that proverb is incorrect or mistranslated. Many of the sayings are, indeed, open to various interpretations, so comments or suggestions from readers will be greatly welcomed.

Primrose Arnander

AUTHOR'S PREFACE 2

2011年から三間過ごしたロンドンでプリムローズとのご縁を得たことは幸運でした。ことわざに込められたユーモアや文化の特性に興味を見出す彼女の役に立ちたいと思いました。日英での同じ意味のことわざを見つけた時の彼女のキラキラ輝く目と生き生きした表情は忘れられません。大学では文化人類学を学び、その後アメリカ、カナダ、イギリスでの生活経験を経て文化の違いの理解と尊重の大切さを痛感する私にとって、ことわざを通じて日本文化への理解と関心を促す作業に関われたことをありがたく思います。

It was a privilege for me to become acquainted with Primrose during my days in London from 2011 to 2014. She is enthusiastically interested in understanding proverbs from around the world, approaching them with respect and a sense of humour. Her sparkling eyes and lively face, so apparent when she finds proverbs in English with the same meanings as those in Japanese, increased my motivation to pursue this project. Since I had studied cultural anthropology at university and have experienced life in the USA, Canada, and the UK, I have realised the importance of understanding each culture with respect. I greatly appreciate this opportunity to work with Primrose and hope that this book will help people to understand Japanese culture.

Ritsuko Yamada Nishimae　　西前　山田　律子

我が物と思えば軽し笠の雪

Waga mono to omoeba karoshi kasa no yuki

As it's on my umbrella, the snow seems light

All his geese are swans

石の上にも三年

Ishi no ue nimo sannen

Three years sitting on a stone

Everything comes to him who waits

捕らぬ狸の皮算用

Toranu tanuki no kawazanyō

Counting the skins before catching any raccoon dogs

To count your chickens before they are hatched

海老で鯛を釣る

Ebi de tai o tsuru

To catch a sea bream with a shrimp

To throw a sprat to catch a mackerel

[sprats are small highly active oily fish]

論より証拠

Ron yori shōko

Proof rather than theory

The proof of the pudding is in the eating

隣の芝は青い

Tonari no shiba wa aoi

The neighbour's grass is green

The grass is always greener on the other side

絵に描いた餅

E ni kaita mochi

A cake drawn in a picture

Pie in the sky

郷に入っては郷に従え

Gō ni ittewa, gō ni shitagae

When in a village, do as the villagers do

When in Rome, do as the Romans do

早起きは三文の徳

Hayaoki wa san mon no toku

Early rising earns three mon [obsolete coins]

The early bird catches the worm

毒を以て毒を制する

Doku o motte doku o seisuru

Counteract poison with poison

Fight fire with fire

寝耳に水

Nemimi ni mizu

Like cold water into a sleeping person's ear

A bolt from the blue

禍を転じて福と為す

Wazawai o tenjite fuku to nasu

Turning misfortune into good luck

Every cloud has a silver lining

たとえ火の中水の中

Tatoe hi no naka, mizu no naka

[To plunge] even into fire, even into water

To go the extra mile

泣き面に蜂

Nakitsura ni hachi

Bees on a weeper's face

Misfortunes never come singly

It never rains but it pours

鬼の居ぬ間に洗濯

Oni no inu ma ni sentaku

When the devil is away it is time for washing

When the cat is away the mice do play

蟹は甲羅に似せて穴を掘る

Kani wa kōra ni nisete ana o horu

The crab digs a hole to fit its carapace

Cut your coat according to your cloth

亭主を尻に敷く

Teishu o shiri ni shiku

To put her husband under her backside

The wife wears the pants

勝って兜の緒を締めよ

Katte kabuto no o o shimeyo

Keep your war-helmet string fastened, even after victory

The battle is won, but the war is not over

紺屋の白袴

Konya no shirabakama

The dyer with a white hakama

The shoemaker's son always goes barefoot

[hakama is a long, pleated skirt-like garment, usually dark, except on special occasions]

残り物には福がある

Nokorimono ni wa fuku ga aru

There is luck in the last piece

A handsome husband and ten thousand a year

[said to whoever takes the last piece on the plate]

女房と畳は新しいほど良い

Nyōbō to tatami wa atarashii hodo yoi

Wives and straw mats - the fresher the better

Youth carries all before it

人の振り見て我が振り直せ

Hito no furi mite waga furi naose

Look at others and correct yourself

Wise men learn from others' faults, fools from their own

瓢箪から駒（が出る）

Hyōtan kara koma [ga deru]

Out of a gourd a pony [comes]

To pull a rabbit out of the hat

頭隠して尻隠さず

Atama kakushite shiri kakusazu

Hide one's head, still showing the backside

To bury one's head in the sand

夫婦喧嘩は犬も食わぬ

Fūfugenka wa inu mo kuwanu

Even a dog does not eat the quarrel of a married couple

Don't get between the hammer and the anvil

猫の首に鈴

Neko no kubi ni suzu

Catch the cat with the bell on its neck

Who will bell the cat?

習うより慣れよ

Narau yori nare yo

Learn from actions rather than from lessons

Experience is the best teacher

飛んで火にいる夏の虫

Tonde hi ni iru natsu no mushi

A summer insect flying into the flame

He sails close to the wind

空き腹にまずい物なし

Sukibara ni mazui mono nashi

Everything tastes delicious to the hungry stomach

Hunger is the best sauce

七度尋ねて人を疑え

Nanatabi tazunete hito o utagae

Check seven times before you suspect anyone

Look before you leap

河豚は食いたし命は惜しし

Fugu wa kuitashi inochi wa oshishi

I'd like to taste a puffer fish, but my life is also dear to me

Honey is sweet but the bee stings

逃がした魚は大きい

Nigashita sakana wa ōkii

The fish that escaped was a big one

The one that got away

[as described by fishermen who 'tell a tall story']

立つ鳥跡を濁さず

Tatsu tori ato o nigosazu

The taking-off bird leaves no mess

The diligent man covers his tracks

大風呂敷を広げる

Ō buroshiki o hirogeru

To spread out a large wrapper

To be full of hot air

All hat and no cattle [American]

二足の草鞋を履く

Nisoku no waraji o haku

To wear two pairs of straw sandals at the same time

To run with the hare and hunt with the hounds

二階から目薬

Nikai kara megusuri

Eye drops falling from upstairs

Wide of the mark

清水の舞台から飛び降りる

Kiyomizu no butai kara tobioriru

Decide to jump down from the Kiyomizu Temple platform

Cross the Rubicon

[no going back – based on Julius Caesar crossing the River Rubicon in 49 BC, thus triggering civil war in Rome]

出る杭は打たれる

Deru kui wa utareru

A protruding nail is hammered down

Don't stick your neck out

蓼食う虫も好き好き

Tade kuu mushi mo sukizuki

There are even bugs that eat knotweed

One man's meat is another man's poison

There is no accounting for tastes

適材適所

Tekizai tekisho

Right wood in the right place

Round peg in a round hole

去る者は日々に疎し

Saru mono wa hibi ni utoshi

Those who depart are forgotten day by day

Out of sight, out of mind

類は友を呼ぶ

Rui wa tomo o yobu

Similarity summons friends

Birds of a feather flock together

酒は百薬の長

Sake wa hyakuyaku no chō

Sake is the best of a hundred medicines

A drop of what you fancy does you good

後は野となれ山となれ

Ato wa no to nare, yama to nare

Afterwards let it be field or mountain

As the tree falls, so must it lie

[*Après moi, le déluge* – French saying]

船頭多くして船山に登る

Sendō ōkushite fune yama ni noboru

Too many boatmen sail the boat up the hill

Too many cooks spoil the broth

虎穴に入らずんば虎子を得ず

Koketsu ni irazunba koji o ezu

If you do not enter a tiger's den, you will catch no cub

Nothing ventured, nothing gained

風前の灯火

Fūzen no tomoshibi

Like a candle before the wind

To hang by a thread

悪銭身に付かず

Akusen mi ni tsukazu

Ill-gotten money does not stay with one long

Crime doesn't pay

身から出た錆

Mi kara deta sabi

Rust from myself [my own sword]

Hoist on his own petard [a medieval catapult used in war]

To shoot oneself in the foot

灯台下暗し

Tōdai moto kurashi

The lighthouse does not shine on its own base

To miss the wood for the trees

開いた口が塞がらない

Aita kuchi ga fusagaranai

Unable to close opened mouth

You could knock me down with a feather [astonished]

羹に懲りて膾を吹く

Atsumono ni korite, namasu o fuku

Having learnt from boiling soup, he blows on fish salad

Once bitten, twice shy

一念岩をも通す
Ichinen iwa omo tōsu

A concentrated mind pierces even a rock

Where there's a will, there's a way

塵も積もれば山となる

Chiri mo tsumoreba yama to naru

Even dust, when piled up, can form a mountain

Many a mickle makes a muckle

庇を貸して母屋を取られる

Hisashi o kashite omoya o torareru

Lend the eaves and the whole building will be taken

Give him an inch and he'll take a mile

一寸の虫にも五分の魂

Issun no mushi nimo gobu no tamashii

Even an insect of one inch has half an inch of spirit

Even a worm will turn

我田引水

Gaden insui

Drawing other people's water into one's own rice fields

Taking care of Number One

生き馬の目を抜く

Ikiuma no me o nuku

To pluck out the eyes of a live horse

He would sell his own grandmother

毒食わば皿まで

Doku kuwaba sara made

If eating poison, eat up plate and all

Hung for a sheep as for a lamb

石橋を叩いて渡る

Ishibashi o tataite wataru

To cross a stone bridge sounding it step by step

To wear belt and braces

Better safe than sorry

一寸先は闇

Issun saki wa yami

One inch ahead in the darkness

What will be, will be

焼け石に水

Yakeishi ni mizu

Water on a hot stone

Save your breath to cool the porridge

弘法筆を選ばず

Kōbō fude o erabazu

Kobo was not choosy about his brushes

A bad workman blames his tools

[Kobo was one of the great Japanese calligraphers]

羽が生えたように売れる

Hane ga haeta yōni ureru

To sell as if wings had grown

To sell like hot cakes

四角な座敷を丸く掃く

Shikaku na zashiki o maruku haku

To sweep a square room in a circle

To cut corners

重箱の隅をつつく

Jūbako no sumi o tsutsuku

To pick out the inside corners of a jubako [lacquered lunch box]

To dot the 'i's and cross the 't's

To split hairs

左団扇で暮らす

Hidariuchiwa de kurasu

To live with a fan in one's left hand

To live the life of Riley

血は水よりも濃い

Chi wa mizu yori mo koi

Blood is thicker than water

(the same in both languages)

縁の下の力持ち

En no shita no chikaramochi

A strong man in the basement

Still waters run deep

武士は食わねど高楊枝

Bushi wa kuwanedo takayōji

A Samurai, even when he has not eaten, uses his toothpick

To put on a brave face

同じ穴の狢

Onaji ana no mujina

Badgers of the same lair

Thick as thieves

目糞鼻糞を笑う

Mekuso hanakuso o warau

Eye dirt sneering at nose dirt

Pot calling the kettle black

犬猿の仲

Kenen no naka

Relations between dog and monkey

Like oil and water

There is no love lost between them

柳の下にいつも泥鰌はいない

Yanagi no shita ni itsumo dojō wa inai

Loaches aren't always found under a willow

Don't push your luck

可愛い子には旅をさせよ

Kawaii ko ni wa tabi o saseyo

If you love your son let him travel

Travel broadens the mind

裾取って肩へつぐ

Suso o totte kata e tsugu

Taking from the hem to patch the shoulder

Robbing Peter to pay Paul

十人十色

Jūnin toiro

Ten men, ten colours

It takes all sorts to make a world

一石二鳥

Isseki nichō

Two birds with one stone

To kill two birds with one stone

餅は餅屋

Mochi wa mochiya

Leave rice cake making to the rice cake maker

Let the shoemaker stick to his last

犬も歩けば棒に当たる

Inu mo arukeba bō ni ataru

The dog that trots about finds a stick

Every dog has its day

逃げるが勝ち

Nigeru ga kachi

Fleeing is winning

Live to fight another day

[*Reculer pour mieux sauter* – a French saying]

馬の耳に念仏

Uma no mimi ni nenbutsu

A sutra [Buddhist prayer] in a horse's ear

Falling on deaf ears

弁慶の泣き所

Benkei no nakidokoro

Benkei's weak point

The Achilles heel

[Benkei was a historic warrior-monk, famous for his invincibility. In Greek mythology, when Thetis dipped her baby son Achilles in the protecting waters of the River Styx, she held him by the heel, which thus remained vulnerable]

陸に上がった河童

Oka ni agatta kappa

A water sprite on the bank

A fish out of water

襤褸は着ても心は錦

Boro wa kite temo kokoro wa nishiki

Though in rags, he has a heart of brocade

Clothes do not make the man

花より団子

Hana yori dango

Dumplings rather than blossoms

Fine words butter no parsnips

高嶺の花

Takane no hana

A flower on lofty heights

[She is] out of my league

盗人を見て縄を綯う

Nusubito o mite nawa o nau

See a thief and make a rope

To shut the stable door after the horse has bolted

釈迦に説法

Shaka ni seppō

Preaching Buddhism to Buddha

Teaching your grandmother to suck eggs

内弁慶

Uchi Benkei

Benkei only at home

Every cock crows on his own dunghill

蛙の面に水

Kaeru no tsura ni mizu

Water on a frog's face

Water off a duck's back

明日の百より今日の五十

Asu no hyaku yori, kyō no gojū

Fifty today rather than a hundred tomorrow

A bird in the hand is worth two in the bush

朝飯前の仕事

Asameshi mae no shigoto

A job before breakfast

It's a piece of cake

[said of a task easily fulfilled]

能ある鷹は爪を隠す

Nō aru taka wa tsume o kakusu

A wise hawk hides its talons

Hold your cards close to your chest

鵜の真似をする烏は水に溺れる

U no mane o suru karasu wa mizu ni oboreru

The crow copying the cormorant is drowned

Don't imitate the fly before you have wings

薮をつついて蛇を出す

Yabu o tsutsuite hebi o dasu

Don't poke a bush [it might drive out a snake]

Let sleeping dogs lie

知らぬが仏

Shiranu ga hotoke

Innocence allows you to be like Buddha

What the eye doesn't see, the heart doesn't grieve over

袖擦り合うも多生の縁

Sode suriau mo tashō no en

Sleeve touches sleeve, as predestined in another life

It's written in the stars

噂をすれば影がさす

Uwasa o sureba kage ga sasu

Talk of a person and you'll see his shadow

Talk of the devil and he is sure to appear

臭い物に蓋をする

Kusai mono ni futa o suru

Cover up a stinking scandal

To sweep under the carpet

To kick into the long grass

[for example, by requesting an Official Enquiry which could end in a 'whitewash']

来年のことを言うと鬼が笑う

Rainen no koto o iu to oni ga warau

Talk of next year and even the ogres will laugh

Man proposes, God disposes

['If you want to make God laugh, tell him your plans' – Woody Allen]

猿も木から落ちる

Saru mo ki kara ochiru

Even a monkey can fall from a tree

Even Homer nods

[The Roman poet Horace referred to the Greek poet Homer becoming drowsy and making mistakes]

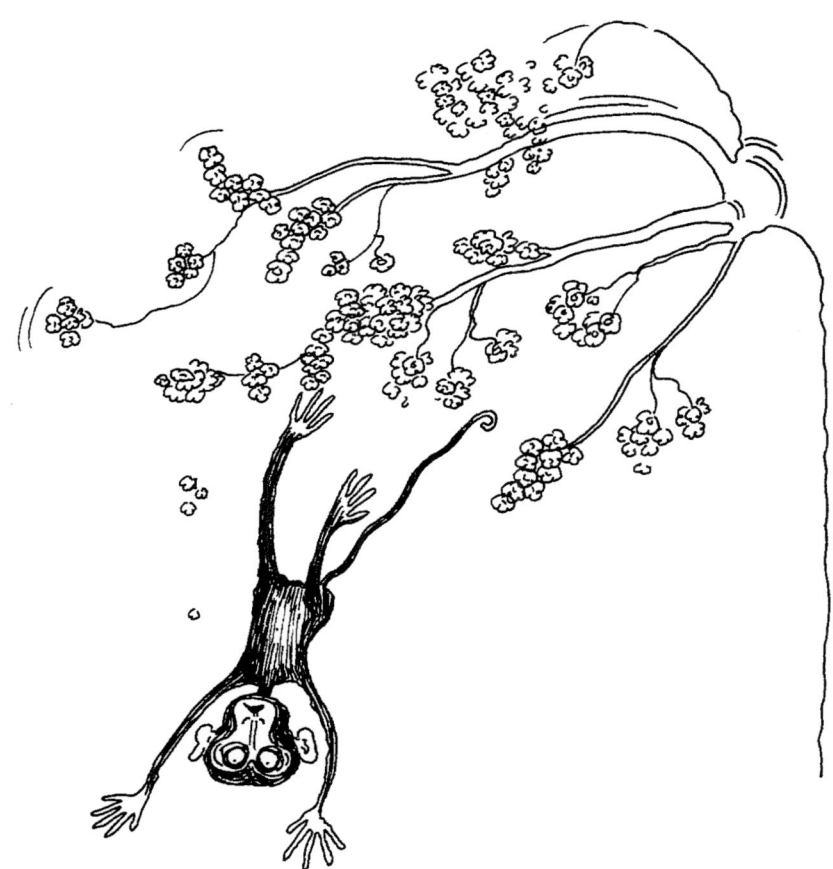

急がば回れ

Isogaba maware

If you are in a hurry, make a detour

Make haste slowly

実る稲穂は頭を垂れる

Minoru inaho wa kōbe o tareru

The head of the abundant rice plant hangs down

To hide your light under a bushel

月とすっぽん

Tsuki to suppon

The moon from the snapping turtle

Chalk and cheese

蛙の子は蛙

Kaeru no ko wa kaeru

The child of a frog is a frog

Like father, like son